Friends

new seasons™

a division of Publications International, Ltd.

Art Resource: Fine Art Photographic Library, London;
Erich Lessing; *Les Muses* **by Maurice Denis/** © 1999 Artists Rights Society (ARS),
New York/ADAGP, Paris; Sharon Broutzas; Planet Art;
Sunrise, Brent at Low Water **by Julian Novorol,**
Private Collection/Bridgeman Art Library, London/New York;
SuperStock; Christie's Images; David David Gallery, Philadelphia;
Eric Isenburger/Private Collection; Tretiakov Gallery, Moscow;
Valder/Tormey/International Stock.

Original inspirations by:
Lain Chroust Ehmann
Jan Goldberg
Marie Jones
Tricia Toney

Compiled inspirations by Joan Loshek

Louis Weber, CEO
Publications International, Ltd.
7373 North Cicero Avenue
Lincolnwood, Illinois 60712

Manufactured in China.

8 7 6 5 4 3 2 1

ISBN: 0-7853-3520-X

Friendship is a magical
vehicle in which two
distinct souls journey
together to different
destinations.

A phone call
from a friend—
a cool drink
on a parched,
dry day.

A letter from a
friend—a break
in the clouds
when the rain
pours down.

A hug from
a friend—
a down-filled
blanket while a
snowstorm rages.

Dreams and
ambitions
take hold
more quickly
when you
share them
with
someone
you love.

True wealth cannot be measured in material objects

or worldly possessions,

but in the depth and quality of our friendships.

Our Photo

My best friend _____ and me.

A friend makes you complete inside. A balance is achieved from two viewpoints, two backgrounds, and two hearts.

A friend is someone who
listens to your dreams,
challenges your fears,
cares for your feelings,
and forgives your
shortcomings.

Come walk with me

through life, my friend,

arm in arm we'll stroll.

With love and hope

to light our path,

and faith to guide our souls.

Always

I may not call to talk with you

as often as I should.

I may not come to visit you

as often as I could.

And even though our busy lives

sometimes keep us apart,

no matter how much time goes by,

you're always in my heart.

A friend is a present you give yourself.

ROBERT LOUIS STEVENSON

To My Friend

The joy of having a friend like you

is a blessing beyond compare.

Our lives are a celebration of

the special bond we share.

The secret to a healthy friendship is for both people to
put more energy into the relationship than they take out.

It's easy to love
a friend for all the
things we have in
common. It's harder,
but much more
valuable, to love the
things that set us apart
from one another.
Learning to appreciate
our differences brings a
new level of intimacy
to our relationships
with others.

No distance of place or lapse of time can
lessen the friendship of those who are
thoroughly persuaded of each other's worth.

ROBERT SOUTHEY

A true friend is someone
who never stops believing
in your dreams, even if you have.

$\mathscr{A}$ friend loves you at all times.
When you aren't looking your best,
a friend insists that you do.
When you don't feel your best,
a friend makes you laugh.

When you worry about your
future, a friend reminds you of
how far you've already come.

You can lean on a friendship on your road to success.

You appreciate that friendship when your friend is

happier about your success than you are.

The day you became my friend, my world became blessed.

With my friend
by my side, I can
conquer all the
challenges of life.

A true friend is one with
whom you can share quiet
moments as comfortably as
raucous celebrations.

Our Photo

When you smile, dear friend, I feel joy in my heart.

Friends make the
best umbrellas,
sheltering us
from the
rainstorms of life.

Support from a friend after trouble

is as welcome as sunshine after a storm.

True friends are like
 marathon runners,
pacing each other
 through the race of life.
When one *stumbles,*
 the other drops
 back to help.
When one surges *forward,*
 the other joins in flight.

Friendships, like gardens, must be nourished and
cultivated if they are to flourish and thrive.
Take time to pull the weeds, turn the soil,
and plant new seeds. Then enjoy the beauty
of this love you have created.

You will discover another part of yourself

in each new friend you make.

A true friend stands on the sidelines of your life,

proudly cheering you on as you win each of life's battles.

A friend is a cheerleader when you win,

a counselor when you lose,

a confidante when you need to share,

a clown when you're feeling blue.

A best friend absorbs half your sadness and amplifies twice your joy.

The quality of a friendship
can be measured
by the amount of silence
the two of you are comfortable
letting pass between you
when you are together.

A loyal and true friend

is a precious,

priceless gift.

Good friends can talk together; great friends can dream together.

When our lives get overloaded, one of the first things
we cut back is the time we spend with friends.
But it is these very relationships that can center us,
ease our stress, and remind us of our true priorities.

Mistakes are valuable. They show us the correct path to take next time.

We look to our friends for different things. Some are "night-on-the-town" friends. Some are telephone friends. Some are office friends. Some are advice friends. Like colorful blossoms, each contributes her unique qualities to a huge bouquet and brings something special to our lives.

Our Photo

My friends and I can go anywhere and have a great time.

When hearts are melancholy
and souls are feeling blue,
there's nothing like the love of friends
to help you make it through.

We pass through seasons in friendships, just as we pass through seasons of the year. Our relationships with others grow, bloom, and sometimes wilt, merely because their time has come. We don't need to regret these passings, for they are a natural part of the earth's movement. Instead, we can look at them with fond recollection, knowing that spring will soon come again.

The rules of a friendship are simple and true:
Do unto your friends as you'd have them do.
Give back to them what they've given to you.
Be there for them as they've been there for you.

Encouraging words and
caring actions are precious
gifts from a friend. We
could live without both of
these things, but our lives
would be incomplete.

We often hesitate to extend help

unless asked.

We don't want to interfere or

overstep our boundaries,

or we are afraid that our behavior

will be misinterpreted.

But an opportunity to assist others

is a rare gift,

and if your actions come

from the heart,

you will never be misjudged.

What a wonderful place the world would be

if we thought of each new person we met

as a friend waiting to be discovered.

When we love our friends,
we see their goodness and beauty,
no matter what they look like,
how old they are, what they choose
to wear. When we learn to recognize
the soul underneath these outward
trappings, our own lives are enriched.

Friends provide the antidote that cures whatever ails us.

Someone to lean on
    when times get too
    tough,
someone to laugh with at
    life's silly stuff,
someone who'll share
    when there's more
    than enough,
that's what a friend
    means to me.

A friend is one who understands

Any loss or gain.

A friend is one who knows your thoughts,

And whose feelings will remain.

A friend is one who encourages you,

And supports all your decisions,

A friend is one who yearns with you,

And can see your grandest visions.

A friend is one who helps you through,

Those long and stressful days.

A friend is one who lifts you up,

In a hundred different ways.

A friend is one who loves you much,

Just the way you are.

A friend is one who's in your heart,

Whether near to you or far.

Best friends share the same vision, but through different sets of eyes.

Enhance your own

    spiritual growth

    by contributing

      to the growth

      of others.

Visiting with old friends is like rereading favorite
books. Though you know the stories by heart,
you are compelled to turn the pages again and again,
reliving the precious memories one more time.

Wishing to be friends is quick work,

but friendship is slow ripening fruit.

ARISTOTLE

Our Photo

During the holidays, I spend time with my friends.
They are family to me.

The world's greatest
treasure
is the small, simple
pleasure
of spending our time
with good friends.
Amidst laughter
and tears
we are bound through
the years
by a loyalty that
never ends.

When you perform service for others,

you do a great service for yourself.

Cherish your friendships as you would your greatest
treasures, for that is exactly what they are.

Every person is
brought into our
lives to teach us
something. As you
see each of your
friends today, ask
yourself what
lessons they hold
for you and what
lessons you might
be teaching them.

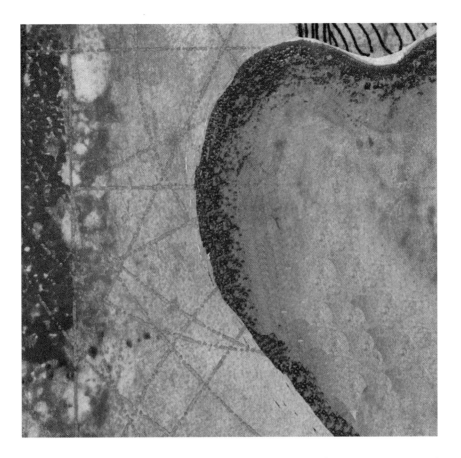

There is in friendship something of all relations,

and something above them all.

It is the golden thread that ties

the heart of all the world.

JOHN EVELYN